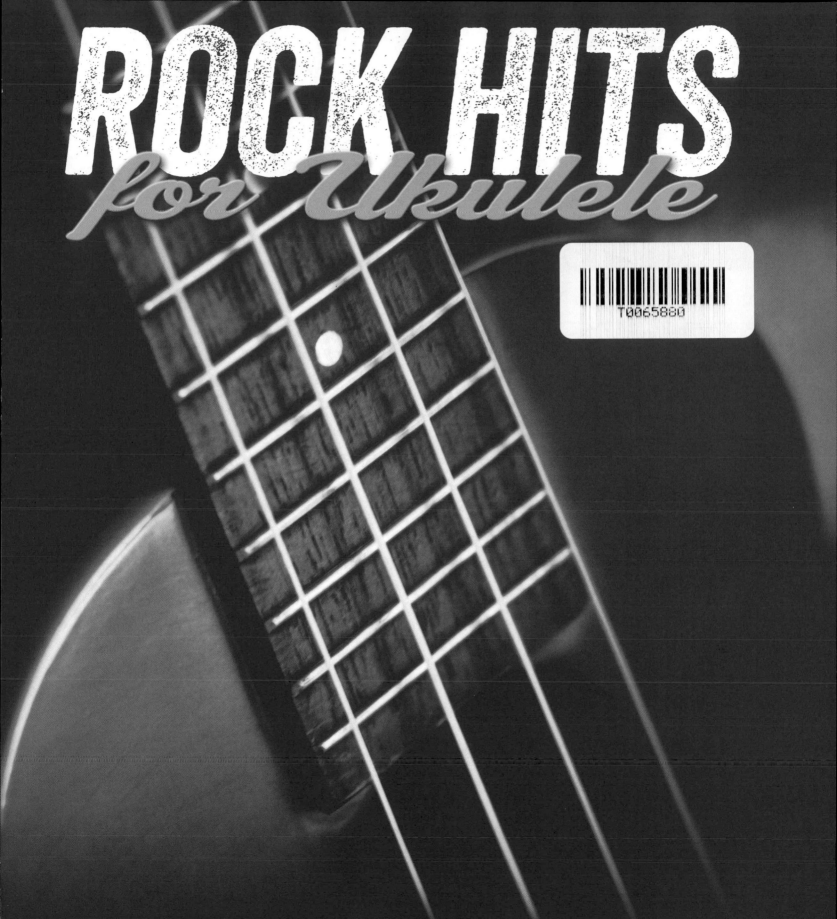

ROCK HITS
for Ukulele

CONTENTS

Better Man

Words and Music by Eddie Vedder

_____ she tells _____ her-self, _____ oh. _____

Mem - 'ries back _____ when she _____ was bold _____

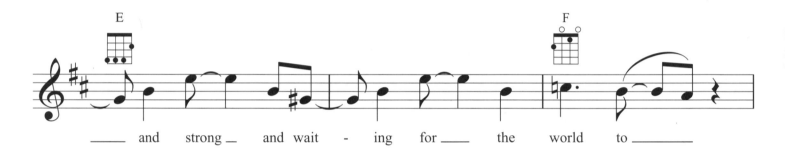

_____ and strong _____ and wait - ing for _____ the world to _____

come a - long. _____ Swears she knew _____ it, now she swears he's gone. _____

Chorus

_____ She lies _____ and says _____ she's in love _____ with him,

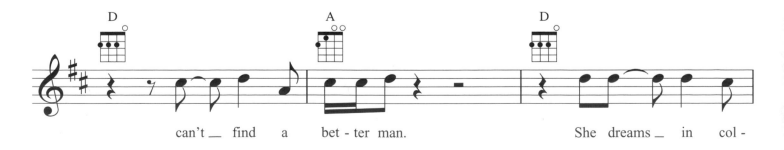

can't _____ find a bet - ter man. She dreams _____ in col-

6

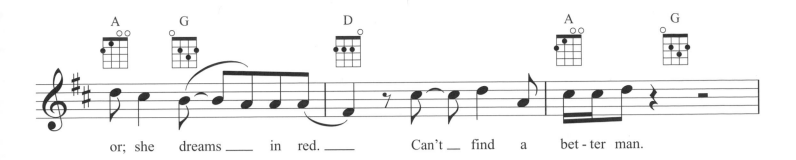

or; she dreams ___ in red. ___   Can't ___ find   a   bet - ter man.

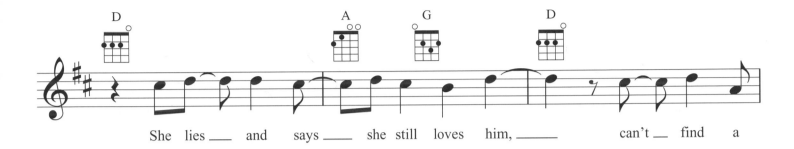

She lies ___ and   says ___ she still loves him, _____ can't ___ find   a

bet - ter man. ___   She dreams _ in col - or; she dreams ___ in red. _

___   Can't ___ find _ a   bet - ter man. _____   Can't ___ find ___ a

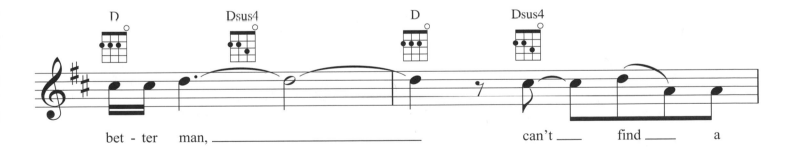

bet - ter man, _____   can't ___ find ___ a

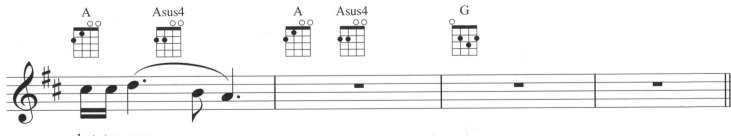

bet - ter man. _____

Breakeven

Words and Music by Stephen Kipner, Andrew Frampton, Daniel O'Donoghue and Mark Sheehan

what am I s'posed to say ___ when I'm all choked up that you're ___ o - kay? _____

To Coda 1

To Coda 2

I'm fall - in' to piec — es, ___ yeah, ___ I'm fall - in' to piec -

D.C. al Coda 1
(take 2nd ending)

- es. ___

3. They

Coda 1   **Interlude**

- es. ___

Bridge

Oh, ___ you got his heart and my heart and none of the pain.

You took your suit - case; I took the blame. Now I'm tryin' to make sense of what lit - tle re - mains, ___

Additional Lyrics

2. Her best days will be some of my worst.
   She finally met a man that's gonna put her first.
   While I'm wide awake, she's no trouble sleepin',
   'Cause when a heart breaks, no, it don't break even.

3. They say bad things happen for a reason,
   But no wise word's gonna stop the bleedin'.
   'Cause she's moved on while I'm still grievin',
   And when a heart breaks, no, it don't break even.

Black Hole Sun

Words and Music by Chris Cornell

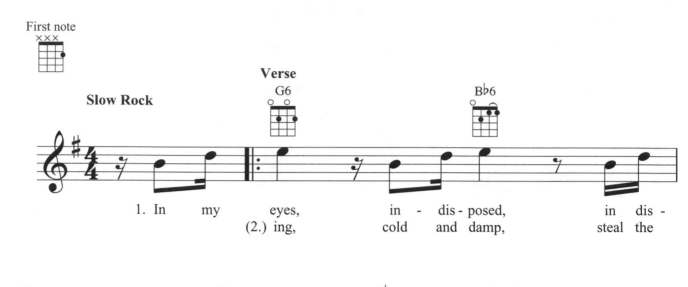

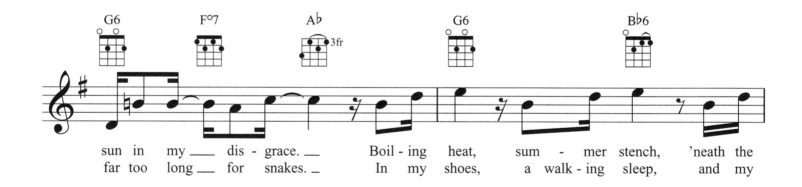

Won't you come? _____

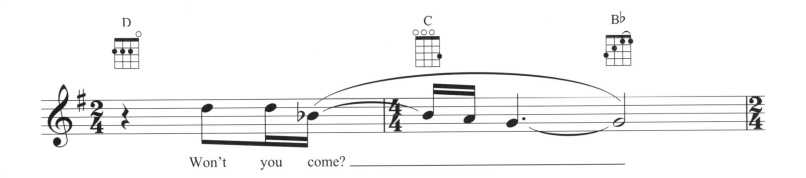

Won't you come? _____

Won't you come? _____

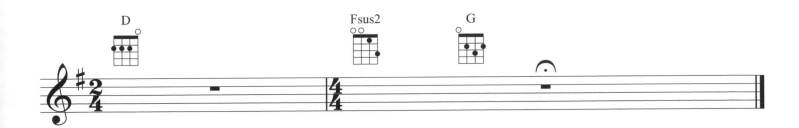

Won't you come? _____

Creep

Words and Music by Albert Hammond, Mike Hazlewood, Thomas Yorke, Jonathan Greenwood, Colin Greenwood, Edward O'Brien and Philip Selway

in a beau-ti-ful world. ___
when I'm not a - round. ___
what - ev - er you want. ___

I wish I were spe -
You're so ver - y spe -
You're so ver - y spe -

- cial;
- cial;
- cial;

you're so ver - y spe - cial.
I wish I were spe - cial.
I wish I were spe - cial.

Chorus

But I'm a creep, ___   I'm a weird -

- o. ___

What the hell ___ am I do - ing here? ___

1.
To Coda

I don't be - long ___ here.

2.

3. I don't care if it hurts; ___ ___ here,   oh, ___

Bridge

_____ oh. _____ She's run - ning out _____ a - gain. _

_____ She's

run - ning out. _____ She run, run, run, run. _____

_____

Run. _____ 5. What - ev - er makes you hap -

Coda

_____ here.   I don't be - long _____ here.

Centuries

Words and Music by Peter Wentz, Patrick Stump, Joseph Trohman, Andrew Hurley, Jonathan Rotem, Suzanne Vega, Justin Tranter, Michael Fonseca and Raja Kumari

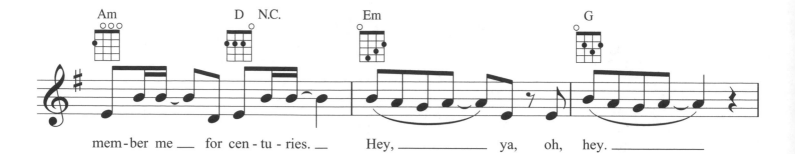

mem-ber me ___ for cen-tu-ries. ___ Hey, _____ ya, oh, hey. _____

Hey, _____ ya, re - mem-ber me ___ for cen-tu-ries. ___

Verse

1. Mum-mi-fied my teen-age dreams. ___ No, it's noth-in' wrong ___ with me. ___ The

kids are all ___ wrong; the sto-ry's all ___ off. Heav-y met-al broke my heart.

Come on, come on and let me in. ___ The bruis-es on your thighs like my fin-ger-prints. ___ And

this is s'posed to match the dark-ness that you felt. I

hey. _____ Hey, _____ ya, re -

Verse

mem - ber me ___ for cen - tu - ries. ___

2. And I can't stop 'til the whole world knows my name, _ 'cause

I was on - ly born in - side my dreams. _ Un - til you die for me, as long as there's a light, my

D.S. al Coda 1

shad - ow's o-ver you 'cause I, I am the op - po-site of am - ne - si - a. _____ And

you're a cher - ry blos - som; you're a - bout to bloom. You look so pret - ty, but you're gone so soon.
Duh, duh,

Coda 1

Bridge

mem - ber me ___ for cen - tu - ries. ___ We've ___ been here for-

22

ev - er, _____ and here's _____ the fro - zen proof.

I _____ could scream for - ev - er; _____ we are _____ the poi - soned

Pre-Chorus

youth. Duh, duh, duh, duh, duh, duh, duh, __ duh, duh, duh, duh, duh, duh, duh, duh, __ duh. Duh, duh,

D.S.S. al Coda 2

duh, duh, duh, duh, duh, __ duh, duh, duh, duh, duh, duh, duh, __ duh. Some

Coda 2

Hey, _____ ya, oh, hey. _____ We'll go down in

his - to - ry, ___ re - mem - ber me ___ for cen - tu - ries. ___

I Will Follow You into the Dark

Words and Music by Benjamin Gibbard

that they both ___ are sat - is - fied, ___ il -

lu - mi - nate ___ the "no's" ___ on their va - can - cy signs; ___ if

there's no one be - side ___ you when your soul ___ em - barks, ___ then

To Coda

1.

I'll fol - low you ___ in - to the dark. 2. In

2. **Verse**

3. You and ___ me ___ have seen ev - 'ry - thing to see, ___

___ from Bang - kok to Cal - ga - ry, and the soles ___ of your shoes ___

are all worn down. The time for sleep is now, but it's noth-ing to cry a-bout, 'cause we'll hold each oth-er soon in the black - est of rooms.

D.S. al Coda

If

Coda

Outro

Then I'll fol - low you in - to the dark.

Additional Lyrics

2. In Catholic school, as vicious as Roman rule,
   I got my knuckles bruised by a lady in black.
   I held my tongue as she told me, "Son,
   Fear is the heart of love." So I never went back.

Do I Wanna Know?

Words by Alex Turner
Music by Arctic Monkeys

'Cause there's this tune _ I found _ that makes _ me think _ of you _ some-how, _ and I

play it on _ re - peat _ un - til I fall _ a - sleep, _

spill - ing _ drinks on _ my set - tee. (Do I wan-

Chorus

- na know?) _ If _ this feel - ing flows _ both ways? _ (Sad to see _

_ you go.) _ Was sort of hop - ing that _ you'd stay. _ (Ba - by, we _

_ both know.) _ Oh, that the nights _ were main - ly made _ for say - ing things _

that you ___ can't say ___ to - mor - row day. ___ Crawl - ing back to

Bridge

you. Ev - er thought of call - ing when ___ you've had a few? _____'Cause I al - ways

do. May - be I'm too _____ bus - y be - ing yours to fall for some -

To Coda

bod - y new. _____ Now I've thought it through. Crawl - ing back to

Verse

N.C.(Gm)

you. 2. So have you ___ got the guts?

Been won - d'rin' if ___ your heart's _ still o - pen, and ___ if so, ___ I wan - na know _

(Eb)   (Cm)

_____ what time _____ it shuts. _____   Sim - mer down   and   puck - er   up. _____

(Gm)

I'm sor-ry   to   in - ter - rupt. _____   It's   just _____   I'm   con - stant - ly   on   the   cusp _____   of _____

(Eb)   (Cm)

_____   try - - - in'   to   kiss _____   you. _____   But   I   don't   know   if _____

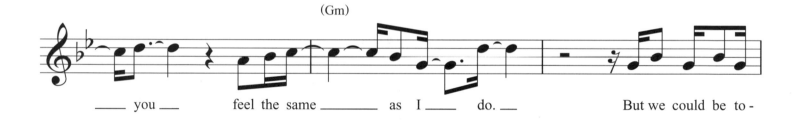
(Gm)

_____   you _____   feel   the   same _____   as   I _____   do. _____   But   we   could   be   to -

(Eb)   (Cm)   (D)   **D.S. al Coda**

geth - er _____   if   you   want - ed   to. _____   (Do   I   wan -

Coda
Gm

Outro-Chorus
Eb

through.   Crawl - ing   back   to   you.   If _____   this   feel -
(Do   I   wan - - na   know?) _____

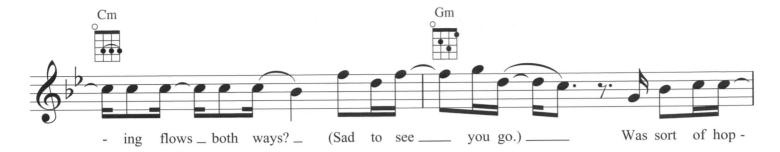

- ing flows _ both ways? _ (Sad to see _ you go.) _ Was sort of hop -

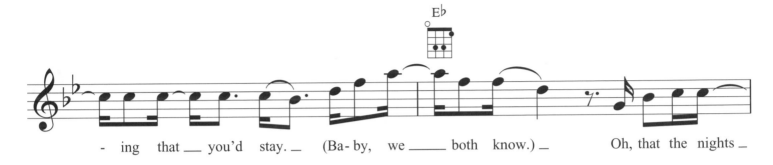

- ing that _ you'd stay. _ (Ba- by, we _ both know.) _ Oh, that the nights _

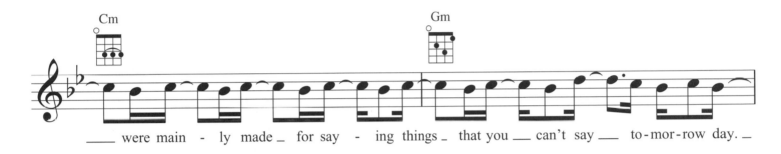

_ were main - ly made _ for say - ing things _ that you _ can't say _ to-mor-row day. _

_ (Do I wan - na know?) _ Too bus-y be - ing

yours to fall. (Sad to see _ you go.) _ Ev-er thought of call - ing, dar - ling? (Do I wan-

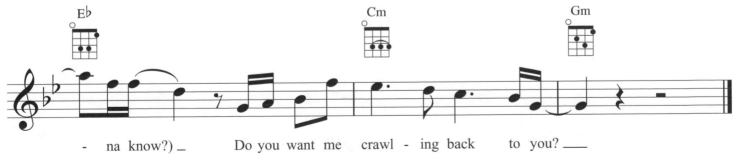

- na know?) _ Do you want me crawl - ing back to you? _

Lonely Boy

Words and Music by Dan Auerbach, Patrick Carney and Brian Burton

1. Well, I'm so a- bove ___ you, and it's plain to see, ___
(2.) ma - ma kept ___ you, but your dad - dy left ___

___ but I came to love ___ you an - y - way. ___
___ you, and I should have done ___ you just the same. ___

___ So you pulled my heart ___ out, and I don't mind _ bleed -
___ But I came to love ___ you. Am I born to ___ bleed

- ing an - y old time you keep ___ me wait - ing, wait - ing,
___ an - y old time you keep ___ me wait - ing, wait - ing,

Paradise

Words and Music by Guy Berryman, Jon Buckland, Will Champion, Chris Martin and Brian Eno

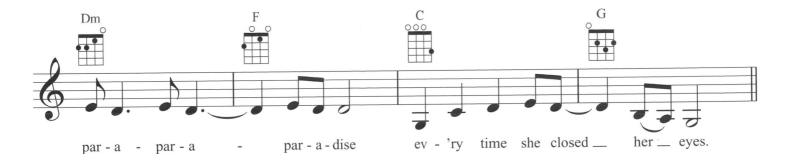

par - a - par - a - par - a - dise   ev - 'ry time she closed ___ her ___ eyes.

Interlude

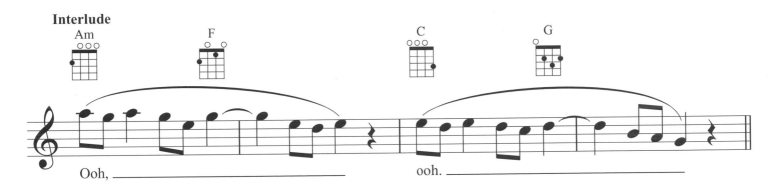

Ooh, _____   ooh. _____

Verse

2. When she was just a girl, _____   she ex - pect - ed the world. ___

_____ But it flew a - way from her reach, _____ and the

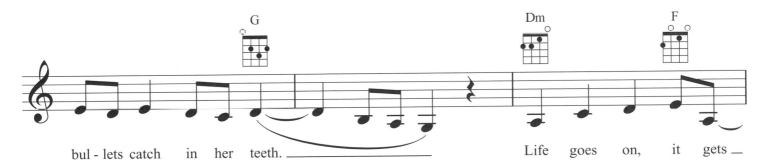

bul - lets catch in her teeth. _____ Life goes on, it gets ___

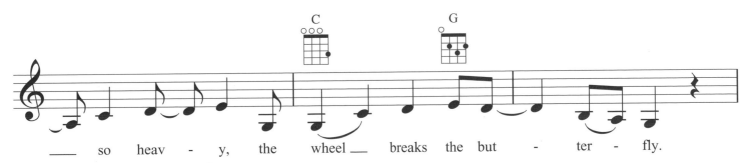

___ so heav - y, the wheel ___ breaks the but - ter - fly.

Ev - 'ry tear, a wa - ter - fall. __ In the night, the storm - y night, __

__ she'll close her __ eyes. _____ In the

night, the storm - y night, __ a - way she'd __ fly _____

Chorus

__ and dream of par - a - par - a - par - a - dise,

par - a - par - a - par - a - dise, par - a - par - a -

- par - a - dise. Oh, _____ oh. _____

She'd dream of

par - a - par - a - par - a - dise, par - a - par - a -

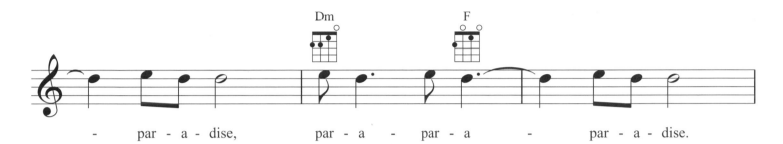

- par - a - dise, par - a - par - a - par - a - dise.

Bridge

Oh, _____ oh. _____ La, la, ___ la, la, la,

la, la, ___ la, la, la, la, la, ___ la, la, la, ___ la, la. ___ And so ly -

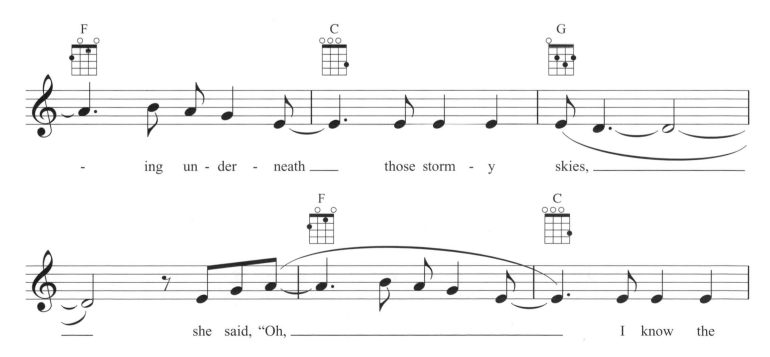

- ing un - der - neath ___ those storm - y skies, _____

she said, "Oh, _____ I know the

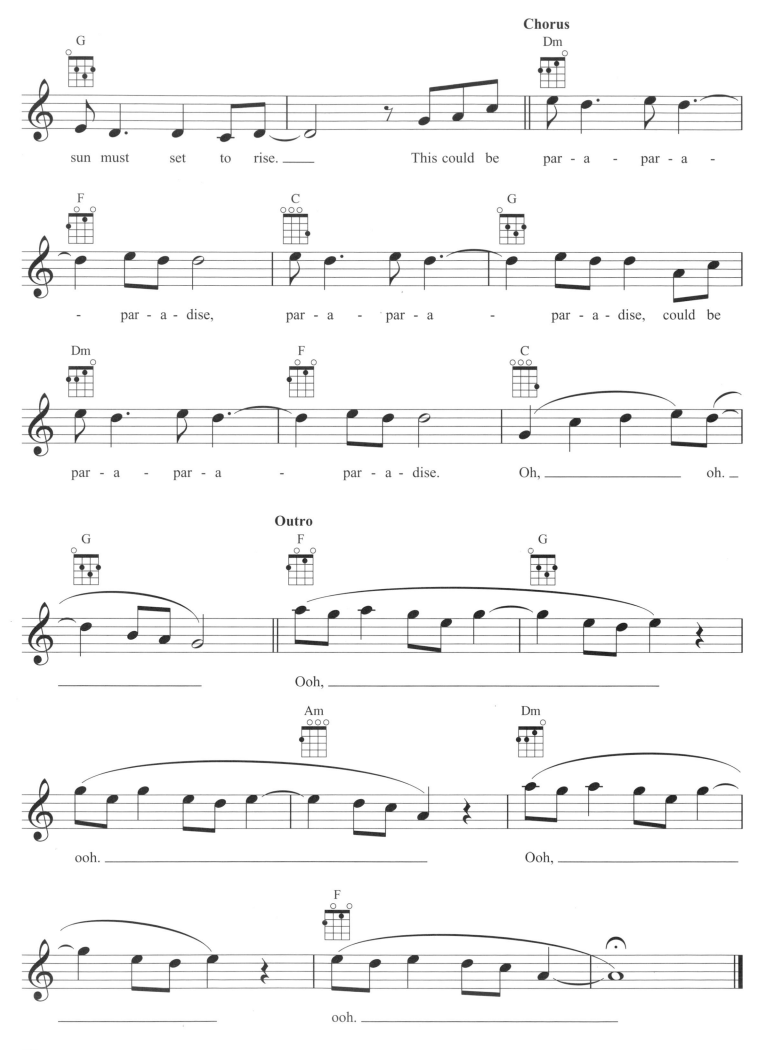

sun must set to rise. _____ This could be par - a - par - a -

- par - a - dise, par - a - par - a - par - a - dise, could be

par - a - par - a - par - a - dise. Oh, _____ oh. _

Outro

_____ Ooh, _____

ooh. _____ Ooh, _____

_____ ooh. _____

The Only Exception

Words and Music by Hayley Williams and Josh Farro

* *Recorded a half step lower.*

Gm6   Fmaj7 5fr   **Chorus** 𝄋 C

love ___ if it does not ___ ex - ist. ___ But, dar - ling, ___ you⟩
(D.S.) You⟩
are ___ the

Gm6   Fmaj7 5fr

on - ly ex - cep - tion.   You   are ___ the   on - ly ex - cep - tion.

C   Gm6   *To Coda* ⊕

You   are ___ the   on - ly ex - cep - tion.   You   are ___ the

Fmaj7 5fr   C

on - ly ex - cep - tion. ___

Verse
C   Gm6

2. May - be I   know, some - where   deep in my   soul, ___ that love nev - er lasts. ___

Fmaj7 5fr   C

___   We've got   to find ___ oth - er ___ ways ___ to make it a -

40

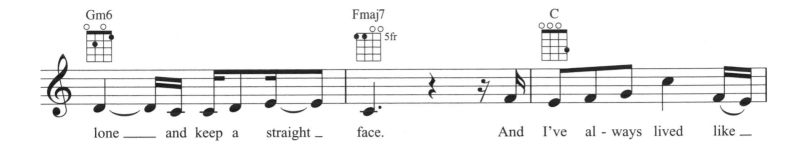

lone ____ and keep a straight ___ face. And I've al - ways lived like ___

this, keep - ing a com - f'ta - ble dis - tance. And

up un - til now, I had sworn ___ to my - self ___ that I'm con - tent ___ with lone - li - ness ___

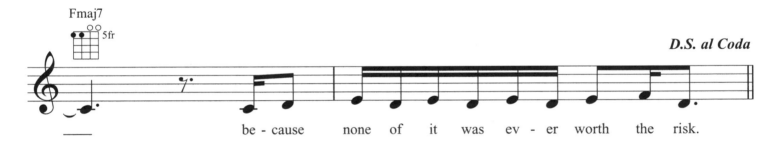

D.S. al Coda

___ be - cause none of it was ev - er worth the risk.

Coda

Bridge

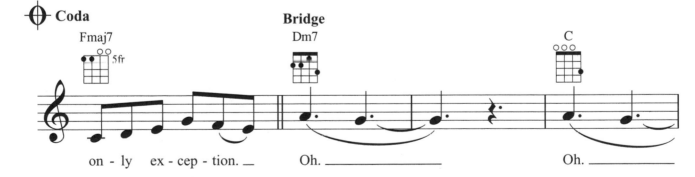

on - ly ex - cep - tion. ___ Oh. _____ Oh. _____

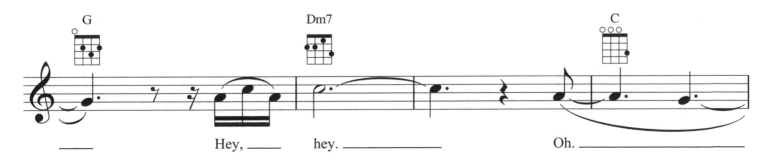

___ Hey, ___ hey. _____ Oh. _____

I've got a tight grip on re - al - i - ty, but I can't let

go of what's in front of me ___ here. _____ I know you're

leav - ing in the morn - ing, when you wake up, leave me

with some kind of proof it's not a dream. ___ Whoa. _____

Chorus

___ You are ___ the on - ly ex - cep - tion.

You are ___ the on - ly ex - cep - tion. You ___ are ___ the

on - ly ex - cep - tion. You are _____ the on - ly ex - cep - tion. _____

Outro-Chorus

You are _____ the on - ly ex - cep - tion. You are _____ the

on - ly ex - cep - tion. You are _____ the on - ly ex - cep - tion.

You are _____ the on - ly ex - cep - tion, and I'm _____ on my

way to be - liev - ing. _____ Oh, _____ and

I'm on my way to be - liev - ing. _____

Plush

Words and Music by Scott Weiland, Dean DeLeo, Robert DeLeo and Eric Kretz

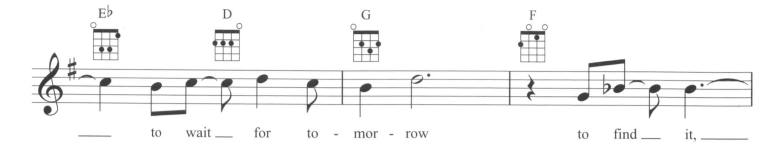

_____ to wait __ for to - mor - row_   _to find __ it, _____

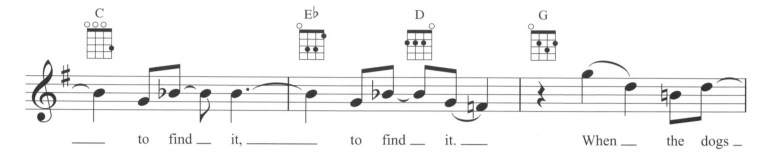

_____ to find __ it, _____   _to find __ it. ____   _When __ the dogs ___

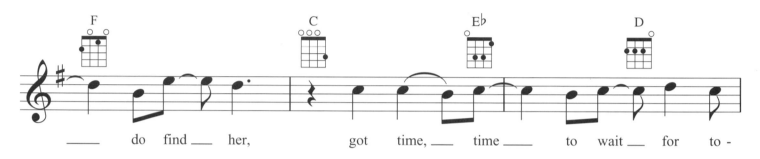

_____ do find __ her,_   _got time, __ time ___ to wait __ for to -_

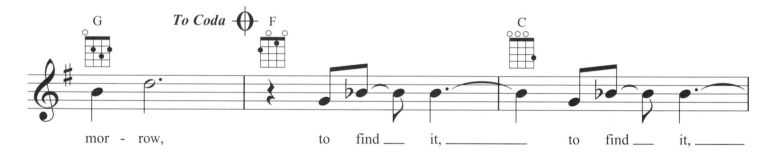

mor - row,   _to find __ it, _____ to find __ it, _____

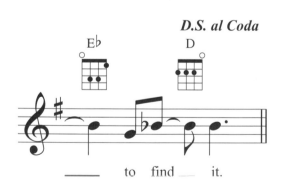

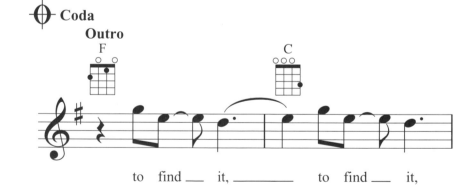

_____ to find __ it._   _to find __ it, _____ to find __ it,_

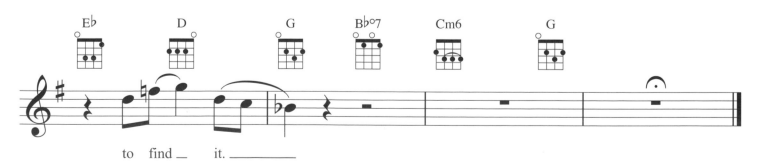

_to find __ it. _____

Radioactive

Words and Music by Daniel Reynolds, Benjamin McKee, Daniel Sermon,
Alexander Grant and Josh Mosser

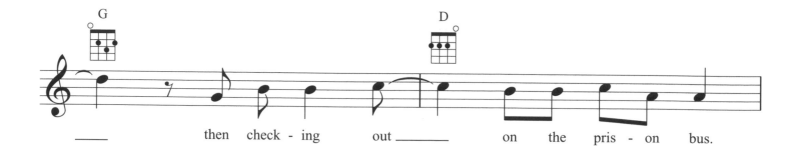

then check - ing out _____ on the pris - on bus.

This is it, _____ the A - poc - a - lypse. _____ Whoa, _____

𝄋 **Chorus**

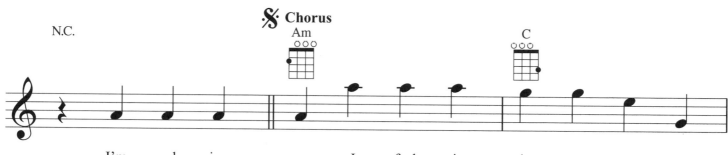

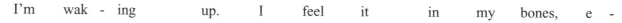

I'm wak - ing up. I feel it in my bones, e -

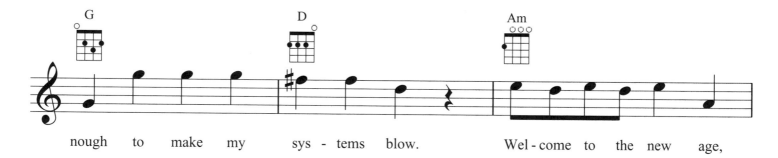

nough to make my sys - tems blow. Wel - come to the new age,

to the new age. Wel - come to the new age, to the new age. _____

_____ Whoa, _____ oh. Whoa, _____ I'm ra - di - o - ac - tive,

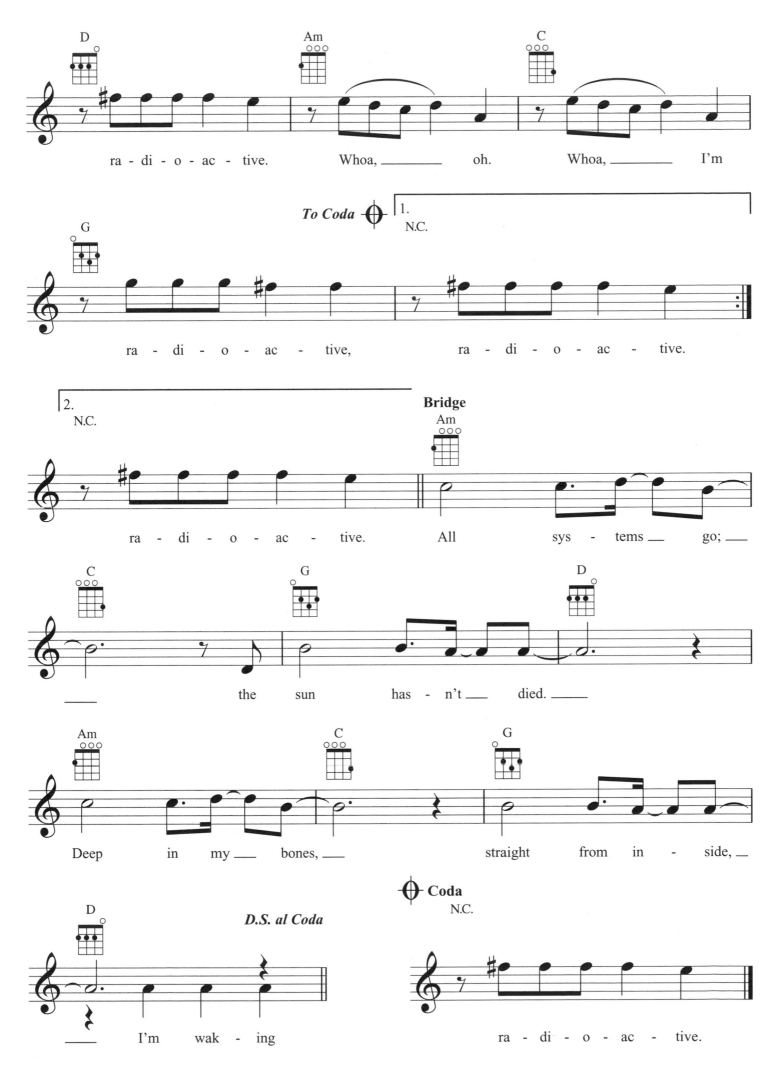

ra - di - o - ac - tive.   Whoa, _____ oh.   Whoa, _____ I'm

To Coda ⊕ | 1.

ra - di - o - ac - tive,   ra - di - o - ac - tive.

2.

ra - di - o - ac - tive.   All   sys - tems __ go; __

__   the   sun   has - n't __ died. _____

Deep   in   my __ bones, __   straight   from   in - side, __

⊕ **Coda**

D.S. al Coda

__   I'm   wak - ing   ra - di - o - ac - tive.

Say It Ain't So

Words and Music by Rivers Cuomo

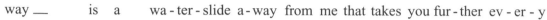

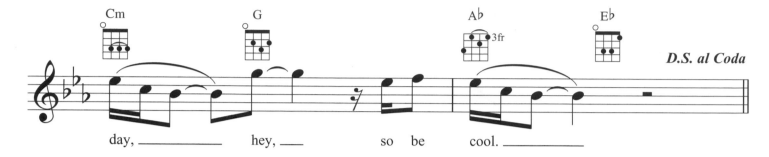

this way __ is a wa-ter-slide a-way from me that takes you fur-ther ev-er-y

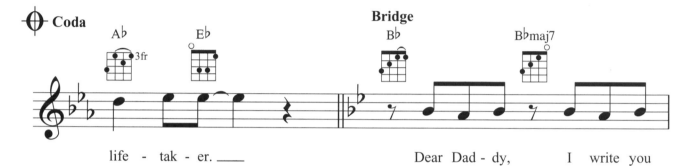

D.S. al Coda

day, _____ hey, __ so be cool. ____

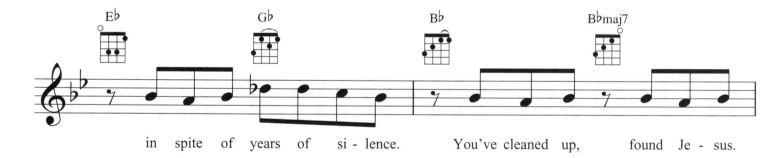

Coda

Bridge

life - tak - er. __

Dear Dad - dy, I write you

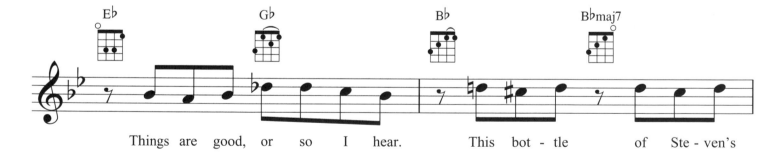

in spite of years of si - lence. You've cleaned up, found Je - sus.

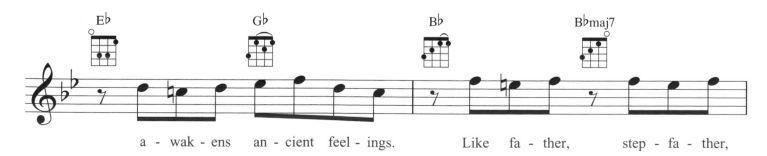

Things are good, or so I hear. This bot - tle of Ste - ven's

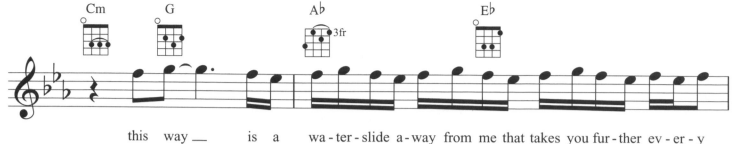

a - wak - ens an - cient feel - ings. Like fa - ther, step - fa - ther,

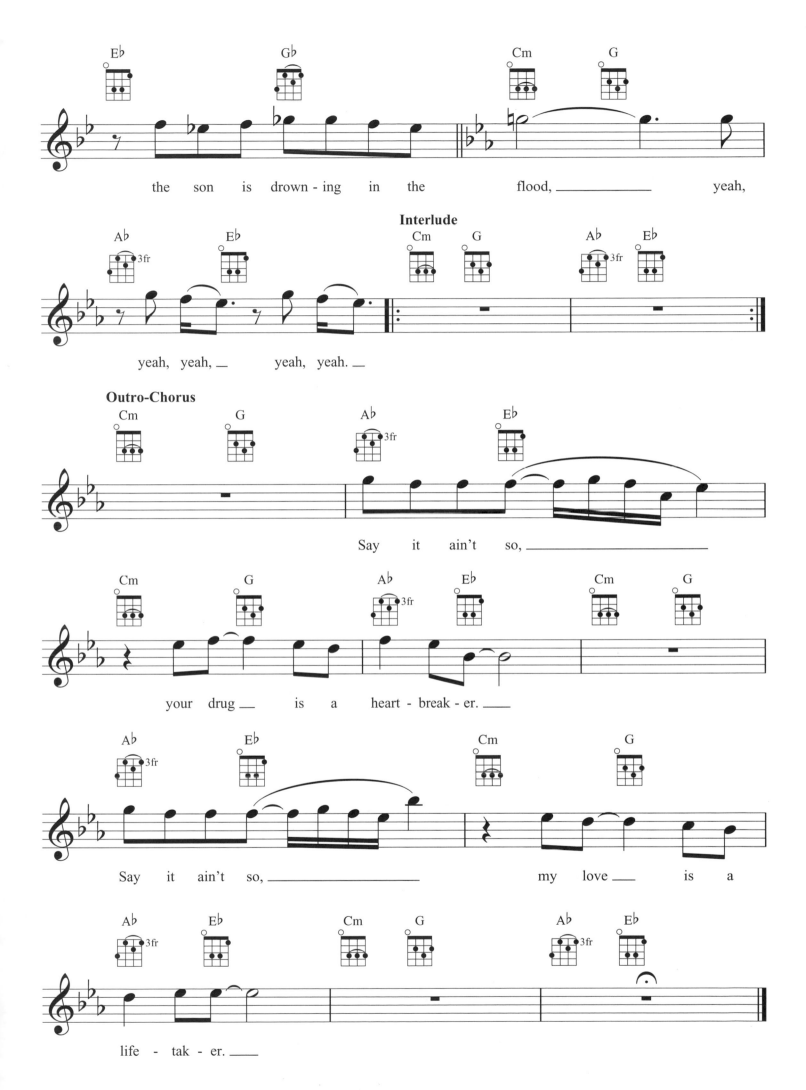

the son is drown - ing in the flood, _____ yeah,

Interlude

yeah, yeah, __ yeah, yeah. __

Outro-Chorus

Say it ain't so, _____

your drug __ is a heart - break - er. ____

Say it ain't so, _____ my love __ is a

life - tak - er. ____

Snow
(Hey Oh)

Words and Music by Anthony Kiedis, Flea, John Frusciante and Chad Smith

Verse
Moderately

1. Come to de-cide that the things that I tried were in my life just to get high on.
2., 3. *See additional lyrics*

When I sit a-lone come get a lit-tle known, but I need more than my-self this time.

Step from the road to the sea to the sky, and I do be-lieve that we re-ly on...

When I lay it on, come get to play it on all my life to sac-ri-fice.

Chorus

1. Hey, oh, ____ lis-ten what I say, ____ oh. _____
2., 3. *See additional lyrics*

I got your hey, oh, ___ now lis - ten what I say, ___

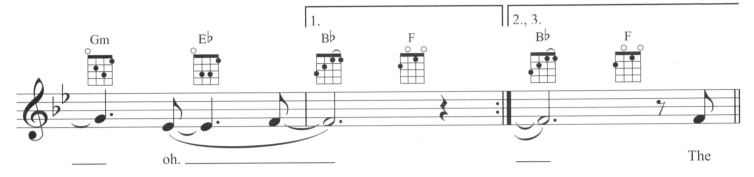

1. oh. _____

2., 3. ___ The

Pre-Chorus

more I see, the less ___ I know, the more ___ I like to let ___ it go.

Hey, _____ oh, whoa. _____

𝄉 Chorus

Deep be - neath the cov - er of an - oth - er per - fect won - der where it's

so ___ white as snow. ___ Pri - vate - ly di - vid - ed by a

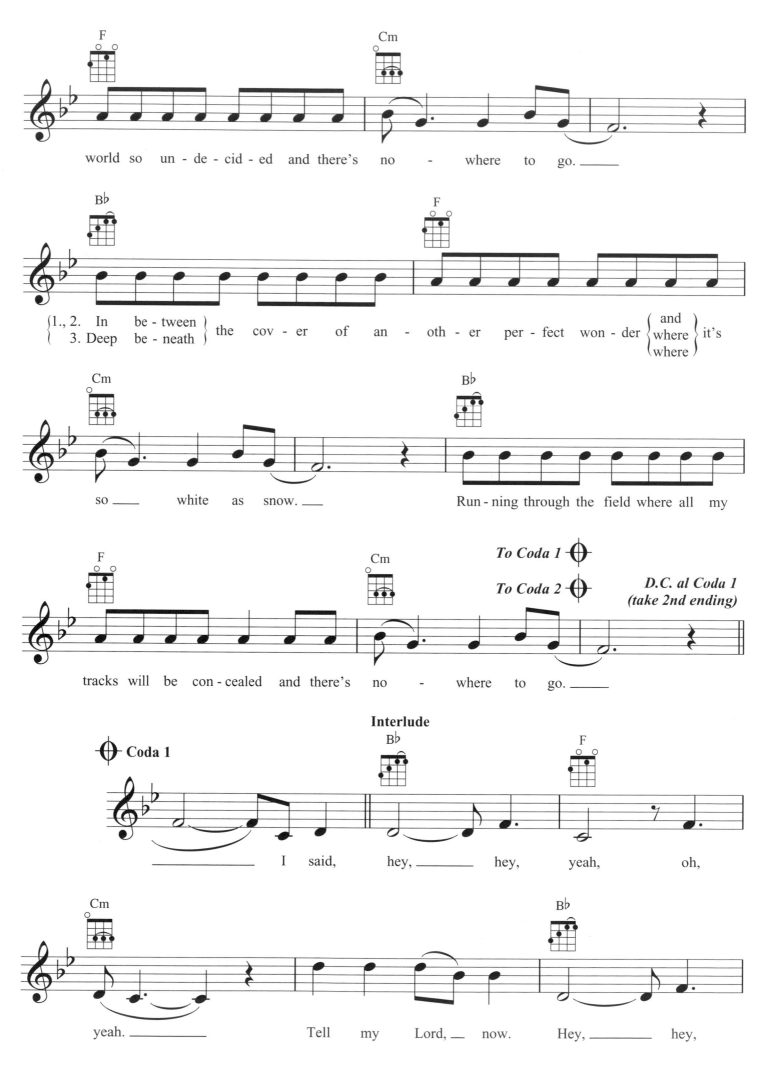

world so un - de - cid - ed and there's no - where to go. ____

{ 1., 2. In be - tween }
{ 3. Deep be - neath } the cov - er of an - oth - er per - fect won - der { and }
{ where } it's
{ where }

so ____ white as snow. ____ Run - ning through the field where all my

To Coda 1

To Coda 2

D.C. al Coda 1 (take 2nd ending)

tracks will be con - cealed and there's no - where to go. ____

Interlude

⊕ **Coda 1**

____ I said, hey, ____ hey, yeah, oh,

yeah. ____ Tell my Lord, ___ now. Hey, ____ hey,

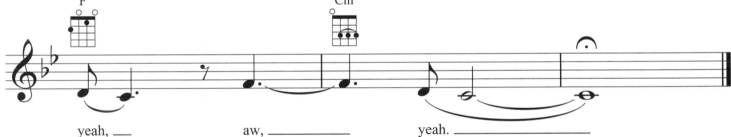

Additional Lyrics

2. When will I know that I really can't go
   To the well once more? Time to decide on
   When it's killing me. When will I really see
   All that I need to look inside?
   Come to believe that I better not leave
   Before I get my chance to ride.
   When it's killing me, what do I really need,
   All that I need to look inside?

Chorus 2: Hey, oh,
   Listen what I say, oh.
   Come back and hey, oh.
   Look at what I say, oh, oh.

3. When to descend to amend for a friend
   All the channels that have broken down?
   Now you bring it up, I'm gonna ring it up
   Just to hear you sing it out.
   Step from the road to the sea to the sky,
   And I do believe what we rely on.
   When I lay it on, come get to play it on,
   All my life to sacrifice.

Chorus 3: Hey, oh,
   Listen what I say, oh.
   I got your hey, oh,
   Listen what I say, oh.

Starlight

Words and Music by Matthew Bellamy

First note

Verse
Moderate Rock

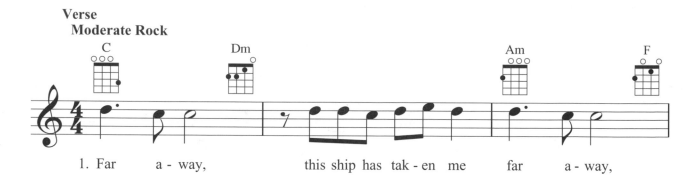

1. Far a - way, this ship has tak - en me far a - way,

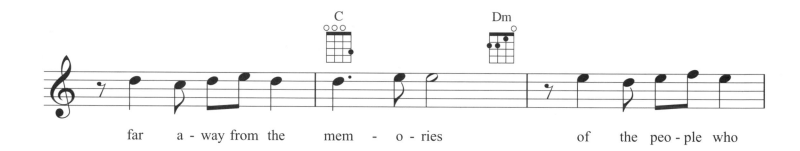

far a - way from the mem - o - ries of the peo - ple who

care if I live or ___ die. ___ Star - light,

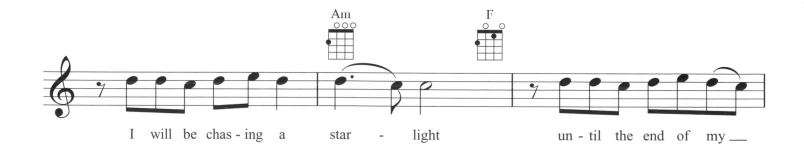

I will be chas - ing a star - light un - til the end of my ___

life. _____ I don't know if it's worth it ___ an - y - more. __

Chorus

_____ Hold _____ you in _____ my __

_____ arms,   I   just want - ed to __ hold _____

To Coda

____ you in _____ my _____ arms.

Verse

2. My _____ life,   you e - lec - tri - fy   my _____ life.
3. Far   a - way,   this ship has tak - en me   far   a - way,

59

C Dm

Let's con-spire to ig - nite _____ all the souls that would
far a - way from the ___ mem - o - ries of the peo-ple who

Am F **Bridge** Dm G7

die just to feel a - live. ___ }
care if I live or ___ die. ___ }
          I'll _____ nev -

E7 Am

- er let ___ you go _____ if you prom - ise not ___ to

B♭ F B♭ E7

fade _____ a - way, ___ nev - er fade _____ a - way. __

Pre-Chorus
Am E7

___ Our hopes ___ and ex - pec -

60

ta - tions, ___ black holes ___ and rev-e-la-

- tions. ___ Our hopes ___ and ex-pec-

ta - tions, ___ black holes ___ and rev-e-la-

1. F   G   2. F

- tions. ___ - tions. ___

G

D.S. al Coda

___

Coda   C   N.C.

I just want-ed to _____ hold... ___

Take Me to Church

Words and Music by Andrew Hozier-Byrne

First note

Verse
Moderate Ballad

1. My lov-er's got hu-mor. She's the gig-gle at a fu-n'ral.

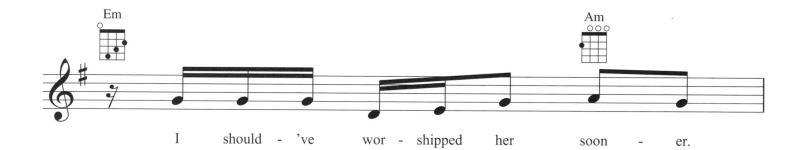

Knows ev-'ry-bod-y's dis-ap-prov-al.

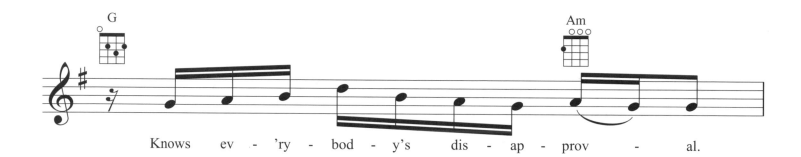

I should-'ve wor-shipped her soon-er.

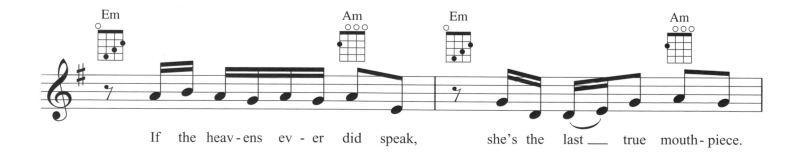

If the heav-ens ev-er did speak, she's the last ___ true mouth-piece.

Ev - 'ry Sun-day's get - ting more bleak, a fresh poi - son each week.

We were born ___ sick; you heard them ___ say it.

My church of - fers no ___ ab - so - lutes. She tells me, "Wor-ship in the bed - room."

The on - ly heav - en I'll be sent to is when I'm a - lone with you.

I was born sick, but I love _ it. Com-mand me to be well. A -

Pre-Chorus

- a - men, a -

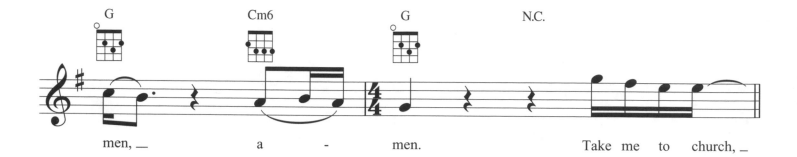

men, ___   a - men.   Take me to church, ___

𝄋 Chorus

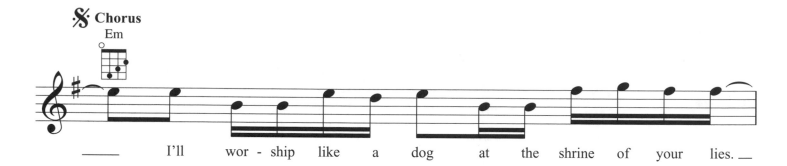

___ I'll wor - ship like a dog at the shrine of your lies. ___

___ I'll tell you my sins ___ and you can sharp - en your knife. ___

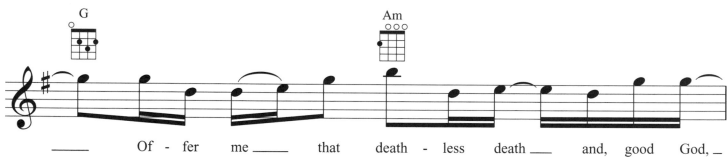

___ Of - fer me ___ that death - less death ___ and, good God, ___

___ let me give you my life.   Take me to church, ___

___ I'll wor - ship like a dog at the shrine of your lies, ___

I'll tell you my sins and you can sharp-en your knife.

Of - fer me that death - less death and, good God,

To Coda 1 / **Verse**

To Coda 2

let me give you my life. 2. If I'm a pa - gan of the good times,

my lov - er's the sun - light. To keep the god - dess on my side,

she de - mands a sac - ri - fice. Drain the whole sea, get some - thing shin - y.

Some - thing meat - y for the main course, that's a fine - look - ing high horse.

mad - ness ___ and soil   of that ___ sad ___ earth - ly scene,   on - ly

then I _____ am ___ hu - man,   on - ly   then   I ____ am ___

Pre-Chorus

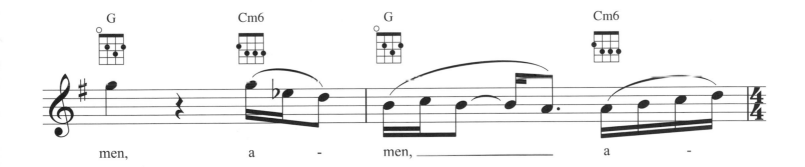

___ clean. _   Oh, _____   oh, _____ a -

men,   a - ___ men, _____   a -

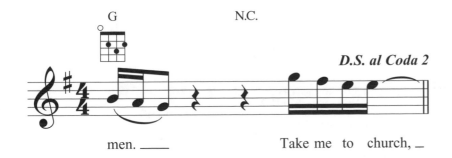

men. ___   Take me to church, _

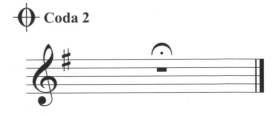

Coda 2

21 Guns

Words and Music by David Bowie, John Phillips, Billie Joe and Green Day

out __ the pride, __ and you look __ for a place __ to hide? __
bro - ken glass, __ and the hang - o - ver does - n't pass. __

Did some-one __ break your heart __ in - side? __ You're in ru - ins. }
Noth-ing's ev - er __ built __ to last; __ you're in ru - ins. }

*Let chord ring

𝄋 **Chorus**

One, twen - ty - one guns, ___ lay down your arms, _

___ give up the fight. _____ One, twen - ty - one guns, _

To Coda ⊕

___ throw up your arms ___ in - to the sky, _____ you and I __

1.
*C

2.
C

_____ *Let chord ring

69

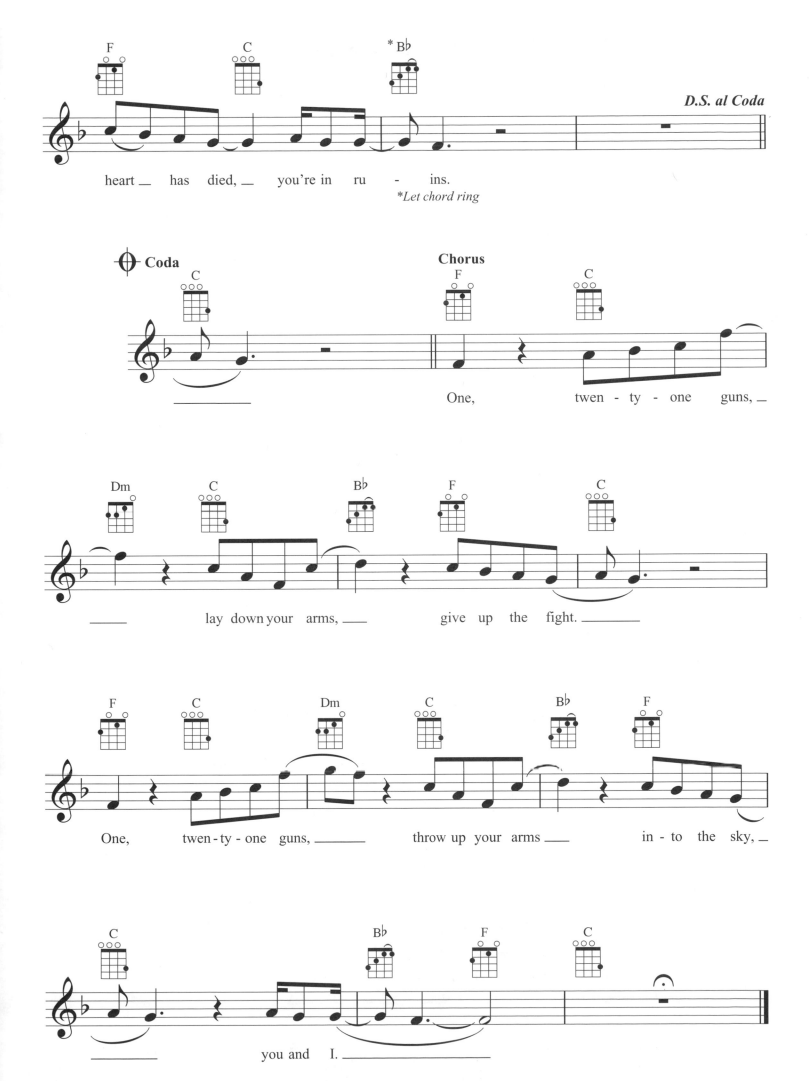

Use Somebody

Words and Music by Caleb Followill, Nathan Followill, Jared Followill and Matthew Followill

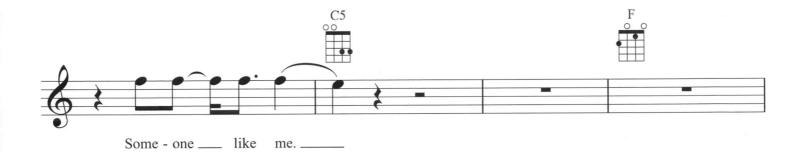

Some - one ___ like   me. ___

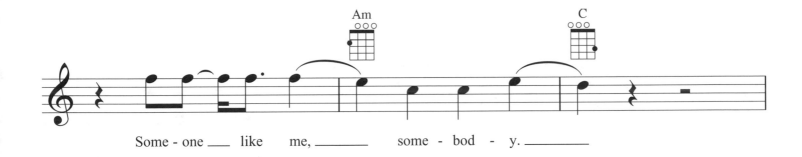

Some - one ___ like   me, ___   some - bod - y. ___

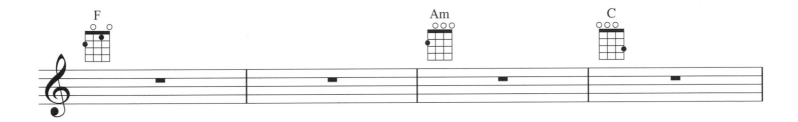

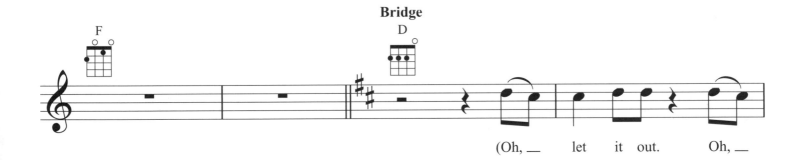

Bridge

(Oh, __   let   it   out.   Oh, __

let   it   out.   Oh, __   let   it   out.   Oh, __   let   it   out.   Oh, __

let   it   out.   Oh, __   let   it   out.   Oh, __   let   it   out.)

We Are Young

Words and Music by Jeff Bhasker, Andrew Dost, Jack Antonoff and Nate Ruess

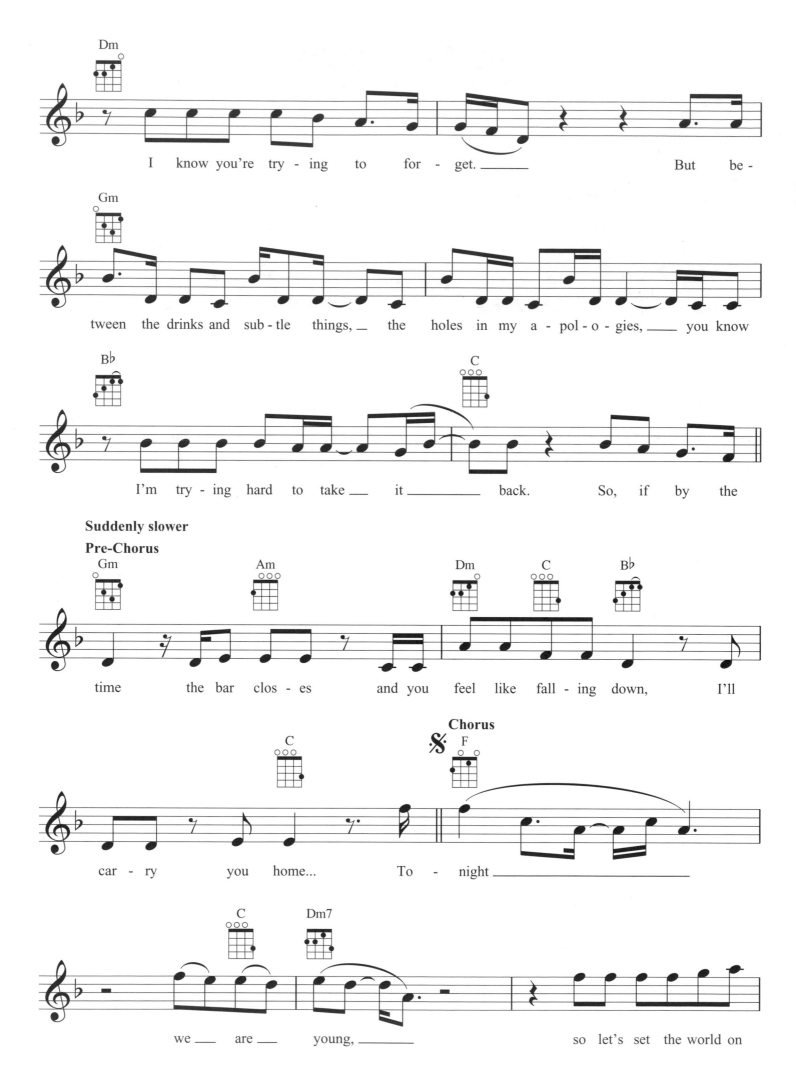

I know you're try-ing to for-get. _____ But be-

tween the drinks and sub-tle things, _ the holes in my a-pol-o-gies, _____ you know

I'm try-ing hard to take _ it _____ back. So, if by the

Suddenly slower
Pre-Chorus

time the bar clos-es and you feel like fall-ing down, I'll

Chorus

car-ry you home... To - night _____

we _ are _ young, _____ so let's set the world on

fi - re; we can burn bright - er than the sun.

To -

night we are

young, so let's set the world on

fi - re; we can burn bright - er than the sun.

To Coda 1

To Coda 2

3. Now I

Male: The moon is on my side; _____ I have no rea - son to run.

So will some - one come and car - ry me home to - night? _

_____ The an - gels nev - er ar - rived, _____ but I can hear the choir. _

D.S. al Coda 2

_____ So will some - one come and car - ry me home? ____ To -

Coda 2

Outro

_____ So, if by the time the bar clos - es and you

feel like fall - ing down, I'll car - ry you home ____ to - night.

Walk

Words and Music by David Grohl, Taylor Hawkins, Christopher Shiflett, Nate Mendel and Pat Smear

think I found __ my place. _____ Can't you feel __

_____ it grow - ing strong - er, lit - tle con - quer - ors? _____

Chorus

_____ Learn-ing to walk __ a - gain. __

I be - lieve __ I've wait - ed long e - nough. Where do I ___

_____ be - gin? _____ Learn - ing to talk __ a - gain. __

_____ I be - lieve _____ I've wait - ed long

e - nough.   Where do I _____ be - gin? _____

Bridge

Now,   for the ver - y first

time,   don't you pay ___ no mind. ___

_____   Set me free ___   a - gain. ___   To

keep a - live a mo - ment at a time,   but   still   in - side   a

whis - per to a ri - ot. To sac - ri - fice,   but know - ing to sur - vive.   The

first to cry an - oth - er state of mind. I'm on my knees, I'm

pray - ing for a sign. For - ev - er, what - ev - er, I nev - er wan - na die. I

nev - er wan - na die. I nev - er wan - na die. I'm on my knees, I

nev - er wan - na die. I'm danc - ing on my grave and

run - ning through the fire. For - ev - er, what - ev - er, I

nev - er wan - na die. I nev - er wan - na leave. I'll nev - er say good - bye. For -

ev - er, what - ev - er. For - ev - er, what - ev - er, oh.

Learn - ing to walk _ a - gain. _ I be - lieve _

_ I've wait - ed long e - nough. Where do I _ be - gin? _

_ Learn - ing to talk _ a - gain. _

Can't you see _ I've wait - ed long e - nough. Where do I _

_ be - gin? _

HAL•LEONARD® UKULELE PLAY-ALONG

AUDIO ACCESS INCLUDED

1. POP HITS
00701451 Book/CD Pack.............$14.99

2. UKE CLASSICS
00701452 Book/CD Pack.............$12.99

3. HAWAIIAN FAVORITES
00701453 Book/CD Pack.............$12.99

4. CHILDREN'S SONGS
00701454 Book/CD Pack.............$12.99

5. CHRISTMAS SONGS
00701696 Book/CD Pack.............$12.99

6. LENNON & MCCARTNEY
00701723 Book/CD Pack.............$12.99

7. DISNEY FAVORITES
00701724 Book/CD Pack.............$12.99

8. CHART HITS
00701745 Book/CD Pack.............$14.99

9. THE SOUND OF MUSIC
00701784 Book/CD Pack.............$12.99

10. MOTOWN
00701964 Book/CD Pack.............$12.99

11. CHRISTMAS STRUMMING
00702458 Book/CD Pack.............$12.99

12. BLUEGRASS FAVORITES
00702584 Book/CD Pack.............$12.99

13. UKULELE SONGS
00702599 Book/CD Pack.............$12.99

14. JOHNNY CASH
00702615 Book/CD Pack.............$14.99

15. COUNTRY CLASSICS
00702834 Book/CD Pack.............$12.99

16. STANDARDS
00702835 Book/CD Pack.............$12.99

17. POP STANDARDS
00702836 Book/CD Pack.............$12.99

18. IRISH SONGS
00703086 Book/CD Pack.............$12.99

19. BLUES STANDARDS
00703087 Book/CD Pack.............$12.99

20. FOLK POP ROCK
00703088 Book/CD Pack.............$12.99

21. HAWAIIAN CLASSICS
00703097 Book/CD Pack.............$12.99

22. ISLAND SONGS
00703098 Book/CD Pack.............$12.99

23. TAYLOR SWIFT – 2ND EDITION
00221966 Book/Online Audio $16.99

24. WINTER WONDERLAND
00101871 Book/CD Pack.............$12.99

25. GREEN DAY
00110398 Book/CD Pack.............$14.99

26. BOB MARLEY
00110399 Book/CD Pack.............$14.99

27. TIN PAN ALLEY
00116358 Book/CD Pack.............$12.99

28. STEVIE WONDER
00116736 Book/CD Pack.............$14.99

29. OVER THE RAINBOW & OTHER FAVORITES
00117076 Book/CD Pack.............$14.99

30. ACOUSTIC SONGS
00122336 Book/CD Pack.............$14.99

31. JASON MRAZ
00124166 Book/CD Pack.............$14.99

32. TOP DOWNLOADS
00127507 Book/CD Pack.............$14.99

33. CLASSICAL THEMES
00127892 Book/Online Audio $14.99

34. CHRISTMAS HITS
00128602 Book/CD Pack.............$14.99

35. SONGS FOR BEGINNERS
00129009 Book/Online Audio $14.99

36. ELVIS PRESLEY HAWAII
00138199 Book/CD Pack.............$14.99

39. GYPSY JAZZ
00146559 Book/Online Audio $14.99

40. TODAY'S HITS
00160845 Book/Online Audio $14.99

Prices, contents, and availability subject to change without notice.